BLAST OFF TO SPACE

BY K.C. KELLEY

AMICUS READERS ● AMICUS INK

amicus
readers

Amicus Readers and Amicus Ink are imprints of Amicus
P.O. Box 1329, Mankato, MN 56002
www.amicuspublishing.us

Library of Congress Cataloging-in-Publication Data

Names: Kelley, K. C., author.
Title: Blast off to space! / by K.C. Kelley.
Description: Mankato, MN : Amicus, [2018] | Series: Amazing adventures
Identifiers: LCCN 2017022594 (print) | LCCN 2017034678 (ebook) | ISBN
    9781681513515 (pdf) | ISBN 9781681513157 (library binding : alk. paper) |
    ISBN 9781681522715 (pbk. : alk. paper)
Subjects: LCSH: Space flight--Juvenile literature. | Readers (Primary) |
    Vocabulary. | Outer space--Exploration--Juvenile literature.
Classification: LCC TL793 (ebook) | LCC TL793 .K432 2018 (print) | DDC
    629.4--dc23
LC record available at https://lccn.loc.gov/2017022594

Editor: Marysa Storm/Megan Peterson
Designer: Patty Kelley
Photo Researcher/Producer: Shoreline Publishing Group LLC

Photo Credits:
Cover: NASA
Dreamstime.com: Pere Sanz 12; Scol22 16T; NASA: 3, 5, 6, 9, 10, 15 (Bill Ingalls), 16R (JPL/Caltech), 16B (ESA/NASA/SOHO).

Printed in China.

HC 10 9 8 7 6 5 4 3 2 1
PB 10 9 8 7 6 5 4 3 2 1

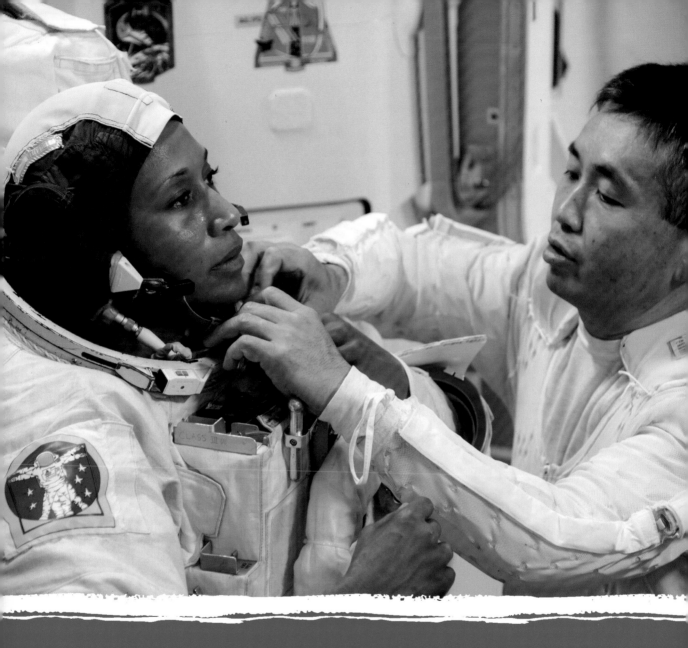

Jean puts on a space suit.
She is going to space!

3, 2, 1. Blast off!
Huge engines roar.
The rocket
zooms up.

The spaceship

reaches space.

It spins

around Earth.

Sam floats in
the spaceship.
There is no
gravity in space!

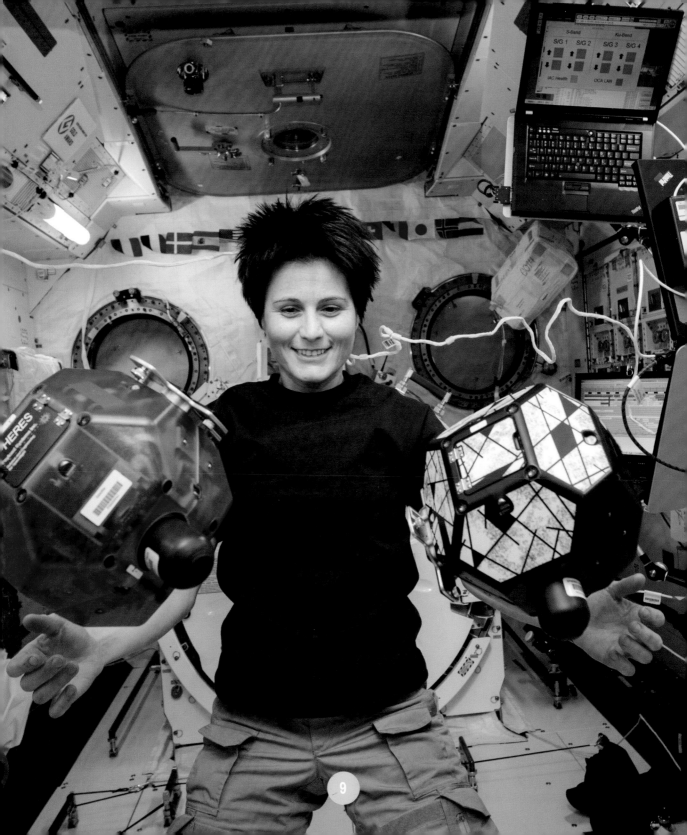

Look at Earth
below!
Mark sees oceans
and clouds.

Now see the stars!
There's the moon, too!

The trip to
space is over.
Welcome home!

SIGHTS IN SPACE

moon

satellite

sun